HOUSE OF ABUNDANCE PUBLICATIONS

The Abyss Below

Astonishing Ocean Facts and Legends. An In-depth Exploration of Our Planet's Watery Realms

The ocean stirs the heart, inspires the imagination, and brings eternal joy to the soul.

WYLAND

Contents

1

Introduction

S tep into the world of wonder and mystery that is our planet's greatest marvel: the ocean. "Into the Abyss: Astonishing Ocean Facts & Legends - An In-depth Exploration of Our Planet's Watery Realms" is more than an ordinary book. It is a journey into the heart of the deep blue, a voyage that promises to captivate, educate, and inspire. It calls to uncover the untamed and unexplored, learn, and dream.

This book unravels the complex tapestry of scientific knowledge, ancient history, and timeless folklore surrounding the world's oceans. It's a deep dive into the grandeur of the oceanic world, from its surface shimmering under the sun's golden touch to its dark abysses, where light fears to tread.

A truly comprehensive resource, this book touches upon the formation of the oceans, their multifaceted roles and functions in our planet's survival, and the dance of life beneath the waves. It is not just a scientific exploration; it is also an adventure into the world of myths and legends, those beguiling tales spun around the ocean's enigmatic depths, capturing the imagination of generations and inspiring countless stories of sea monsters, lost cities, and fabled treasures.

Importance of Oceans in Our World

Imagine a world without oceans. It's hard. That's because oceans are the lifeblood of our planet. The vast blue seas, covering over 70% of Earth's surface, are the heartbeats of life as we know it. They serve as the largest habitat in the world. In this home, diverse species of all sizes and shapes reside, from the microscopic plankton to the majestic blue whale. Many of these species remain unknown, their secrets safely locked away in unexplored depths.

Oceans are a global thermostat, governing the Earth's climate, influencing weather patterns, and nurturing life on a grand scale. They absorb carbon dioxide, producing oxygen, making every other breath we take a gift from the ocean. They are the veins of our planet, circulating currents of water that transport heat, determining the climate of the world's continents.

They are the arteries of global trade and commerce, pathways for ships carrying goods across nations. Yet, despite their undeniable importance, our understanding of these grand bodies of water is just a drop in the ocean. Our knowledge has yet to plunge into the depths of the seas to uncover the many mysteries within their depths.

This book is a testament to the majesty of our oceans, the very cradle of life. It is a call to every reader to appreciate, learn, and protect our oceans, our planet's most priceless resource, a world within our world that remains largely unexplored and misunderstood. Through its pages, we invite you to embark on this voyage of discovery, unlock the secrets of the ocean, and in the process, discover more about our extraordinary planet and ourselves.

2

An Oceanic Overview

Explanation of Terms: The Ocean and The Sea

As we embark on this oceanic journey, it's vital to grasp the words that serve as our navigational aids. When we speak of 'the ocean' or 'the sea,' we often refer to the vast, interconnected expanse of saltwater that swathes over two-thirds of our planet's surface. This is not a singular, solitary entity but a complex system comprising the Atlantic, Pacific, Indian, Southern, and Arctic Oceans.

These terms, though frequently used interchangeably, do carry nuanced differences. A 'sea' is typically a smaller body of water, partially or entirely encompassed by land. Names like the North, Red, or Mediterranean Sea immediately come to mind. However, the distinction between 'seas' and 'oceans' is not razor-sharp. It's a gradient rather than a strict partition, a spectrum of marine environments defined by their sizes, geographic features, and ecological attributes.

One general rule of thumb is that seas are smaller than oceans and are often partially (as marginal seas) or entirely (as inland seas) bordered by land. So, while every sea is part of the ocean, not every aspect of the ocean is a sea. This distinction may seem subtle, but it's a fundamental part of understanding the complexity and variety within the world's water bodies. As we journey across the world's oceans, this understanding will help us appreciate the diverse landscapes and ecosystems that vary from the open ocean's vast expanses to the sheltered coastlines of our world's seas.

The ocean and sea play more than just a physical role; they also have a cultural one. In British English, for instance, 'the sea' is often the term of choice, irrespective of whether the reference is to a specific ocean. These linguistic peculiarities reflect our human perceptions and interpretations of the natural world and add another layer of richness to our exploration of the watery kingdoms.

Exploration of the World Ocean Concept

Once we've grappled with the seas and oceans' distinctions, we'll explore a concept that reframes our understanding of these bodies of water - the 'World Ocean.' This term, coined in the early 20th century by the visionary Russian oceanographer Yuly Shokalsky, encapsulates the idea of a singular, interconnected body of salt water that covers and embraces most of Earth. The 'World Ocean' is not simply a body of water; it is a living, breathing entity that influences everything from the climate to the air we breathe.

This concept underscores the oceans' vastness and connectivity, emphasizing the seamless interchange among its constituent parts. Understanding our global ocean as an interconnected entity rather than disjointed water sections is fundamental to grasping the dynamics of oceanographic processes. It helps us visualize how currents circulate nutrients, how changes in one area can affect remote parts of the world, and how the oceans collectively moderate global climate patterns.

As we plunge into the ocean's mysteries, we must hold onto this perspective of unity and connectivity. Each wave that crashes onto the shore, every creature we will encounter in the depths, is part of this greater whole of the World Ocean. Recognizing this is significant for scientific understanding; it's a poignant reminder of our shared responsibility. The health of any single part of the ocean impacts the entire body's well-being. Therefore, we must see every action taken toward ocean conservation as a step in safeguarding this invaluable, interconnected ecosystem. As we voyage further 'Into the Abyss,' we carry this collective consciousness, realizing our intrinsic link to the ocean's fate and our vital role in its preservation.

3

The Etymology of 'Ocean'

Historical Origin of the Term 'Ocean'

In Chapter 2, we embark on a linguistic journey, tracing the roots of the term 'ocean' back to ancient times. This journey is not merely an etymological exploration; it also unveils how our ancestors viewed the vast water surrounding them and influenced their civilizations.

The word 'ocean' draws its origin from ancient Greek mythology and language, specifically from the figure in classical antiquity, Oceanus. Recognized as the elder of the Titans in classical Greek mythology, Oceanus personified the enormous river believed to encircle the world. This belief not only influenced the term we use today but also reveals how the ancient Greeks and Romans perceived their world - as an island surrounded by an enormous, all-encompassing body of water.

Moreover, Oceanus was often depicted with a dragon tail, a significant mythological motif in its own right. Dragons, as mythical creatures, are usually associated with the primal forces of nature, embodying power, mystery, and often a certain degree of danger or chaos. By associating the ocean with such a powerful symbol, the ancient Greeks captured its dual nature—its capacity to nurture life and its potential for destruction.

But our exploration continues beyond there. The etymology of the word 'ocean' reveals deeper connections across cultures. The concept of Oceanus has been linked to the Indo-European language family, one of the most widely spoken linguistic groups globally. The Greek' Ōkeanós' has been compared to the Vedic epithet ā-śáyāna-, which was attributed to the dragon Vṛtra-, who captured the cows/rivers in ancient Indian mythology.

This interconnectedness of linguistic and mythological references paints a vivid picture of how the concept of the ocean has transcended cultural boundaries and stood the test of time. This common thread may suggest a shared linguistic ancestry and a universal recognition of the ocean's significance and omnipresence in our lives.

The origin of the word 'ocean' takes us back in time, making us realize that our fascination and reverence for the vast waters are as old as civilization. As we explore, let's carry with us this profound sense of shared history and the understanding that our bond with the ocean is truly ancient. We're not just exploring a body of water; we're diving into a symbol that has been revered and mythologized by our ancestors, a symbol that connects us all as residents of this blue planet.

The Indo-European Connection

After immersing ourselves in the mythology of ancient Greece, we transition to an exploration of the broader Indo-European connections to the term 'ocean.' The Indo-European languages, spanning multiple continents and cultures, share a common linguistic root. This shared heritage is reflected in language and myths, legends, and perceptions about the natural world, including the ocean.

The dragon, also a common symbol across Indo-European cultures, often represents the forces of nature, and in this context, it is used to depict the encapsulation and control of water bodies. This points to understanding the ocean (and large water bodies) as entities of immense power that nurture and constrain life. They provide resources but also set boundaries, much like the dragon that hoards treasures or controls rivers.

The fascinating connection between Greek 'Ōkeanós' and Vedic' ā-śáyāna-' opens up a wider discussion about how different cultures perceive and represent the ocean. Though geographically separated, these shared linguistic and mythological motifs reveal a collective human understanding of the ocean's power and importance. These common threads weave together a tapestry that reflects our shared human journey with the sea, a testament to the enduring bond between humanity and our planet's watery depths.

In uncovering these linguistic and mythological connections, we begin to appreciate the importance of our relationship with the ocean and its importance to our shared human story. This shared heritage invites us to view the ocean not merely as a physical entity but as a cultural and psychological symbol that continues to shape our worldview.

4

Origin of Water and Formation of the Ocean

Theories on the Origin of Water on Earth

As we look deeper into the heart of our planet's history, we uncover the captivating mystery of how water, the lifeblood of our world, came into existence. Theories abound, each proposing fascinating perspectives and drawing upon diverse fields of study, from astronomy to geology.

There is consensus among scientists that a significant quantity of water would have been present in the material that formed Earth. Still, the exact processes that led to the abundant oceans we see today are subjects of ongoing investigation and debate. As we embark on this exploration, we'll dive into the concept of atmospheric escape, which postulates that water molecules would have escaped Earth's gravity more easily when our planet was less massive during its formation.

We'll also consider the intriguing possibility that Earth may have had magma oceans during its early days of planetary formation. An early atmosphere of carbon dioxide, nitrogen, and water vapor is believed to have formed through the processes of outgassing, volcanic activity, and meteorite impacts. Over millions of years, as Earth's surface cooled, this water vapor would have condensed to form our planet's first oceans.

Picture an Earth where the oceans might have been significantly hotter than today and perhaps even green due to high iron content. Such conjectures provoke our imagination and underscore the elaborate and dynamic history of water on Earth. This journey into the past also offers us valuable insights into the potential existence and form of water on other planets, further expanding the horizons of our understanding.

The Process of Earth's Formation and the Role of Water

A dive into the process of Earth's formation will allow us to uncover the vital role that water has played in shaping our world from its infancy. Earth's formation was a fiery, turbulent process characterized by a massive, rotating disc of dust and gas that slowly coalesced to form our planet. As part of this process, Earth underwent a phase covered in a sea of molten rock.

Water's role might seem elusive amid this fiery world, but it was integral. Scientists theorize that water may have been present in the rocks and minerals that formed Earth, locked away in their crystalline structures. As the Earth cooled and solidified, these water molecules were released, eventually creating the oceans we see today.

Interestingly, it's also believed that a significant portion of Earth's water came from outer space. As our young planet was battered by a steady barrage of comets and meteorites, these cosmic bodies—many of which contained ice—delivered substantial water to our world.

As we explore these theories, we'll discuss the ongoing debates and the scientific evidence that supports each viewpoint. We'll also discuss the fascinating geological evidence that helps scientists constrain the time frame for liquid water on Earth.

This chapter provides an enlightening look at the origins of our oceans and a broader understanding of how our planet was formed, emphasizing the vital and ever-present role that water has played in the story of Earth. Understanding this intricate history is crucial in appreciating the complex interplay of elements that have led to the Earth as we know it today.

The Early Atmosphere of Earth and the Formation of the First Oceans: An Evolutionary Perspective

Earth, our remarkable home in the vast expanse of the cosmos, has witnessed an extraordinary journey from its fiery birth to the world teeming with the life we know today. Central to this journey has been the evolution of water and the formation of oceans. This chapter aims to illuminate the role of geological and atmospheric processes in shaping the Earth's hydrosphere.

A Prelude to Formation

The role of volcanic activity and meteorite impacts in the

genesis of Earth's early atmosphere cannot be overstated. These cataclysmic events released a cocktail of gases into the young Earth's atmosphere, primarily composed of carbon dioxide, nitrogen, and water vapor.

The Cooling of Earth and the Birth of the First Oceans: As Earth transitioned from a turbulent world of molten rock to a cooler, more stable entity, conditions began to favor the accumulation of liquid water. The transformation was far from overnight - we are talking about a process that unfolded over millions of years. As the Earth's surface cooled, water vapor trapped in the atmosphere began to condense, and rain started to fall. Over millennia, these rains filled the Earth's depressions, giving birth to the first oceans.

An Alien Seascape: An Imaginative Dive into the Past: One might picture the early oceans as vast, serene bodies of blue just as we see them today, but the reality might have been quite different. Imagine instead seas of a greenish tint, significantly hotter than those we're accustomed to. The reason? High iron content in the waters and a substantially warmer global climate.

Understanding how past oceans differed from today's oceans takes us one step closer to fully appreciating our planet's dynamic and ever-evolving nature. The Journey of Water: From Then to Now: As we trace the journey of water through Earth's history, we come to appreciate its integral role in the evolution of life and the shaping of our planet. From the early rains that filled depressions on Earth's surface to form the first oceans to the ice ages that altered sea levels and shaped our current coastlines, water has been a central character in the life narrative on Earth.

This exploration of the early Earth's atmosphere and the formation of the first oceans is more than just a voyage into the past; it's a journey of understanding the world as it is today. By understanding the genesis of our oceans, we can better appreciate the beauty and complexity of the current marine ecosystems and more accurately predict the future of our planet's watery realms.

Geological Evidence for the Existence of Water on Earth

The existence of water on Earth has been a topic of interest and rigorous investigation by scientists. Unraveling the Earth's past requires detective work of a different kind, with rocks and minerals providing the clues necessary to piece together the history of water on our planet.

The Ancient Witnesses

Rocks - Basalt pillows and the Isua Greenstone Belt: Some of the oldest geological formations on Earth, like basalt pillows and the Isua Greenstone Belt, bear evidence of water's long history on our planet. These structures were formed underwater during volcanic eruptions, providing indisputable evidence that liquid water existed on Earth's surface 3.8 billion years ago.

The Nuvvuagittuq Greenstone Belt

Providing a Glimpse into the Primeval Earth: This geological formation, located in Quebec, Canada, is another window into the early Earth. Rocks here have been dated at an astonishing 4.28 billion years old, reinforcing the theory of water's longstanding presence on our planet.

The Limitations and Challenges of Geological Evidence

Despite the invaluable insights that these geological formations provide, their interpretation is challenging. Earth's dynamic nature means that much of the geological record may have been erased or altered by plate tectonics and erosion. Yet, our evidence suggests that our oceans may have existed in some form since the planet's formation.

This section aims to underscore the significance of geological evidence in determining the history of water on Earth. These ancient stones whisper tales of our world's infancy, and the journey water has embarked on since those early epochs. Through their testimony, we understand more deeply our planet's history and the origin of our life-sustaining oceans.

5

The Ocean's Role in Planetary Formation

The Impact of the Ocean on the Hadean Eon

Navigating the depths of time, we embark on a mesmerizing journey into the Hadean eon, a tumultuous period that witnessed the fiery birth of our planet. Earth was a seething cauldron of volcanic activity and relentless meteorite bombardment during this era. Yet, amidst this chaos, the foundations of our oceans were laid. We will explore how the cooling of the Earth's surface allowed water to condense and gather, eventually giving rise to the vast primordial oceans that shaped the course of our planet's evolution. From the Hadean eon emerged the primordial cradle of life. In this mesmerizing era, water played a defining role in shaping the destiny of our world.

How Oceans Might Have Influenced the Emergence of Life

In the early stages of Earth's history, the oceans held the key to the origin and development of life. These vast bodies of water acted as nurturing crucibles, providing an ideal environment for the emergence of the building blocks of life. We will explore how the oceans might have served as fertile breeding grounds for forming complex organic molecules and the evolution of life forms. From the ancient "primordial soup" to the earliest microorganisms that thrived in these watery atmospheres, we will discover how the oceans played a pivotal role in catalyzing the miracle of life on Earth.

Continuous Change and Adaptation

Casting our gaze upon today's oceans, we come to appreciate their dynamic and ever-changing nature. The ebb and flow of tides, the ceaseless movement of currents, and the interplay of wind and wave paint a vivid portrait of the oceans as living entities intertwined with the Earth's systems. In this section, we will embark on a mesmerizing expedition of the dance of oceanic movements. From the mighty global currents that circulate heat and nutrients across the planet to the mesmerizing beauty of localized phenomena such as upwellings and thermohaline circulation, we will uncover the inner workings of this vibrant aquatic world. We will also delve into the impact of plate tectonics, which, over millennia, have sculpted the ocean basins, shaped the continents, and influenced the configuration of our planet's watery domains.

Additionally, The world ocean, a vast interconnected network of water that spans the globe, is in a perpetual state of transformation due to the relentless forces of geology. Coastlines, the delicate meeting points between land and sea, constantly change as tectonic plates shift, mountains rise and erode, and sea levels fluctuate. Erosion by waves, currents, and wind carves away at rocky cliffs and reshapes sandy shores, while sediment deposition builds new landforms. Subduction zones, where one tectonic plate dives beneath another, give rise to volcanic activity and the creation of islands and island chains. The world ocean's structure is also influenced by seafloor spreading. New crust forms at mid-ocean ridges, expanding the ocean basin over time. These ongoing geological processes leave an indelible mark on the coastline and structure of the world ocean, reminding us of the dynamic nature of our planet and the ever-changing interplay between land and sea.

Past, Present, and Future Oceans

Looking back across the vast tapestry of Earth's history, we witness the mesmerizing story of our oceans. From the ancient Panthalassa, the vast ocean that once surrounded the supercontinent Pangaea, to the familiar configuration of the Atlantic, Pacific, Indian, Southern, and Arctic Oceans that grace our modern maps, the oceans have undergone a remarkable transformation journey. This section will guide us through the evolutionary timeline of our oceans, tracing their changing boundaries, their shifting currents, and the impact they have had on shaping the Earth's climate. Moreover, we will peer into the future, contemplating the challenges ahead. Rising sea levels, ocean acidification, and the implications of climate change pose formidable threats to the delicate balance of our oceans. By understanding the past and present dynamics, we equip ourselves with the knowledge needed to navigate the future and strive for the sustainable stewardship of these precious nautical landscapes.

The Ocean's Unending Story

In concluding this chapter, we find ourselves humbled by the significance of the oceans in the grand narrative of our planet s existence. From their enigmatic origins in the Hadean eon to their indispensable role in nurturing life and shaping the Earth's climate, the oceans stand as resolute custodians of our planet's destiny. As we reflect on the mesmerizing journey through the ocean's role in planetary formation, we are filled with awe and wonder for these vast and majestic bodies of water. Their timeless allure beckons us to embrace our collective responsibility to preserve and protect them, ensuring that future generations may continue to be inspired by their beauty, enriched by their resources, and humbled by their importance in sustaining life on Earth.

6

The Ocean in the Climate System

The Role of the Ocean in Colder and Warmer Periods

E xploring the relationship between the ocean and the climate system, we embark on a journey of how the sea greatly influences Earth's climate during both colder and warmer periods. Throughout Earth's history, the ocean has acted as a crucial regulator, absorbing and storing vast amounts of heat and serving as a primary driver of climate patterns. We will journey through time, examining the ocean's pivotal role in shaping climatic conditions during ice ages, when massive ice sheets covered the land and sea levels were lower. We will also investigate how the ocean responds to and influences climate dynamics during warmer periods, such as interglacial periods, when ice sheets retreat, sea levels rise, and the Earth experiences heightened temperatures. Understanding the ocean's role in these climatic shifts is essential for unraveling the mysteries of the past and comprehending the potential implications of current and future climate change scenarios.

Next, we will explore how the ocean's currents and circulation patterns are pivotal in redistributing heat around the planet. The mighty ocean currents, such as the Gulf Stream and the Kuroshio Current, act as conveyor belts, transporting warm and cold waters across vast distances. These currents influence regional climate patterns and have far-reaching effects on global climate dynamics. We will discover the mechanisms behind these currents, examining the role of wind patterns, temperature variations, and salinity changes in driving their motion. By understanding the complex dance of oceanic circulation, we gain a deeper appreciation for the ocean's vital role in modulating Earth's climate, regulating temperatures, and shaping weather patterns.

Ocean as a Carbon Sink

Beyond its role in heat distribution, the ocean is a crucial player in the global carbon cycle. The ocean absorbs and stores massive amounts of carbon dioxide through various physical and biological processes, effectively acting as a carbon sink. We will investigate how the ocean's capacity to sequester carbon helps to mitigate the impacts of greenhouse gas emissions, buffering the effects of climate change to some extent. However, we will also research the potential consequences of this process, such as ocean acidification, as increased carbon dioxide levels alter the delicate balance of marine ecosystems.

Feedback Mechanisms and Climate Change

The complex relationship between the ocean and the climate system involves feedback mechanisms that can either amplify or dampen climate change. We examine the various feedback loops at play, such as the ice-albedo feedback and the influence of ocean temperatures on atmospheric circulation. By comprehending these feedback mechanisms, we can better understand the potential consequences of anthropogenic climate change on the ocean's dynamics and the cascading effects on global climate patterns.

Additionally, we reflect on the critical role of the ocean in building climate resilience. Understanding the sophisticated interactions between the sea and the climate system is essential for effective climate modeling, prediction, and adaptation strategies. By recognizing the ocean's resilience as a natural climate regulator and protector, we gain insights into how we can work in harmony with this vast aquatic realm to mitigate the impacts of climate change and foster a more sustainable future for both the planet and ourselves.

Effects of Glaciers and Ice Caps on Ocean Levels

Glaciers and ice caps, majestic icy giants that adorn our planet's polar regions and high mountain ranges, significantly influence global ocean levels. In this section, we will probe into the dynamics between these frozen reservoirs and the world's oceans, exploring their role in shaping sea levels and the delicate equilibrium of our planet's climate system.

Glaciers and ice caps are immense accumulations of ice formed from compacted snowfall over thousands of years. They represent vast stores of freshwater that have accumulated on land rather than directly in the oceans. We will discuss how these frozen reservoirs act as natural regulators, storing freshwater during colder periods and releasing it during warmer periods.

As the Earth's climate warms, glaciers, and ice caps melt at an accelerated pace. This process contributes to the gradual rise in global sea levels. We also discuss the various mechanisms by which melting ice from glaciers and ice caps enters the ocean, including surface meltwater runoff, calving of icebergs, and the collapse of ice shelves. Through these processes, once stored or land, freshwater finds its way into the world's oceans, resulting in a measurable increase in sea levels.

The effects of melting glaciers and ice caps on ocean levels are not uniform globally. We examine how sea-level changes caused by melting ice can vary regionally, influenced by geographic location, ice thickness, and local climate conditions. Furthermore, we will explore the broader implications of rising sea levels on coastal communities, vulnerable ecosystems, and global climate patterns.

The melting of glaciers and ice caps is linked to climate change through feedback loops. As the ice melts and exposes darker surfaces, such as rock or ocean water, the lower albedo leads to increased absorption of solar radiation, further enhancing the warming effect. We will dig into these feedback processes, studying their role in expediting ice melt and the ensuing elevation of sea levels.

While the effects of melting glaciers and ice caps on ocean levels are significant, they also have far-reaching consequences beyond sea level rise. The freshwater released into the oceans can impact ocean currents, salinity levels, and the delicate balance of marine ecosystems. We will investigate these implications and the potential domino effects on global climate patterns.

By understanding the complex relationship between melting glaciers, ice caps, and ocean levels, we gain insights into the interplay between Earth's cryosphere and hydrosphere. Recognizing the importance of these frozen reservoirs in shaping the delicate equilibrium of our planet's climate system, we can strive for sustainable practices and collective efforts to mitigate the impacts of climate change and protect the future of our oceans and coastal communities.

The Influence of the Ocean on Earth's Atmosphere and Climate

The vast expanse of the ocean not only shapes the Earth's surface but also influences the atmosphere and climate. In this section, we will explore the relationship between the ocean and the Earth's atmospheric conditions, unveiling the ocean's key roles in regulating weather patterns, atmospheric circulation, and the overall stability of our planet's climate system.

The ocean is a massive heat reservoir, storing and releasing vast amounts of thermal energy. Warm ocean currents carry heat from the equator to higher latitudes, moderating temperatures and shaping weather systems. Conversely, cooler ocean currents transport cold water, impacting regional climates and forming distinct climate zones.

Water Vapor and the Water Cycle

The ocean is a primary driver of the Earth's water cycle, which plays a vital role in regulating the distribution of water vapor in the atmosphere. Water is constantly cycled between the ocean, the atmosphere, and land through evaporation, transpiration, and condensation. We will explore how the ocean's vast surface area and water vapor capacity influence cloud formation, precipitation patterns, and the overall humidity of the atmosphere.

Ocean-Atmosphere Interactions

The interface between the ocean and the atmosphere is a dynamic zone where energy, gases, and particles exchange. We will delve into the mechanisms behind these interactions, such as the transfer of gases like oxygen and carbon dioxide and the sale of aerosols and nutrients. These interactions influence air quality, atmospheric composition, and the overall balance of greenhouse gases, playing a crucial role in shaping Earth s climate.

El Niño and La Niña

The tropical Pacific Ocean plays a pivotal role in driving global climate variability through phenomena like El Niño and La Niña. These climate oscillations, influenced by oceanic and atmospheric interactions, have far-reaching impacts on weather patterns, temperature anomalies, and precipitation worldwide.

By unraveling the influence of the ocean on Earth's atmosphere and climate, we gain a deeper appreciation for the intercon-

26

nectedness of our planet's systems. Understanding the ocean's role as a climate regulator, water vapor distributor, and carbon sink allows us to comprehend the delicate balance that sustains our climate and weather patterns. Through this knowledge, we can better understand the potential consequences of human activities on the ocean and strive for sustainable practices that protect the health and resilience of our oceans and the atmosphere.

7

Geography of the Oceans

A View of Earth as a 'Water World' or 'Ocean World'

Embarking on a captivating exploration of the Earth's watery territories, we explore the awe-inspiring geography of the oceans. As we gaze upon our planet from a cosmic perspective, we are struck by its remarkable characteristic as a "water world" or "ocean world." In this section, we immerse ourselves in the breathtaking realization that more than 70% of Earth's surface is covered by the vast expanse of the oceans. We contemplate the profound implications of this abundant presence of water, acknowledging the oceans as the dominant feature that defines the very essence of our planet.

Boundaries and Divisions

Navigating the expansive blue horizons, we encounter the diverse and distinct divisions that characterize the world ocean. We dig into the geographical delineation of the major oceanic basins, including the Atlantic, Pacific, Indian, Southern, and Arctic Oceans. These vast bodies of water have unique characteristics, currents, and ecosystems, shaping the lives and experiences of those who dwell along their shores.

Seas, Marginal Seas, and Inland Seas

Beyond the expansive oceanic basins, we encounter a rich tapestry of smaller bodies of seawater. These include seas, marginal seas, and inland seas, which add a remarkable diversity to the Earth's watery landscape. We examine the characteristics differentiating seas from oceans, appreciating their partially or fully enclosed nature, often bordered by land. We uncover the unique features of famous seas such as the Mediterranean, Red Sea, and Baltic Sea and their vital contributions to regional ecosystems, maritime trade, and cultural heritage. Moreover, we delve into the fascinating world of marginal seas, which lie at the edges of continents, and inland seas, partially enclosed by landmasses, unfolding the captivating stories they tell about Earth's geological and geographical evolution.

The Continental Shelf - Where the Ocean Meets Dry Land

A significant feature of the ocean's geography is the continental shelf, the transition zone where the vast expanse of the sea meets the solid ground. We study the geological and geographical characteristics of the continental shelf, appreciating its relative shallowness compared to the open ocean. We examine the importance of this region as a habitat for diverse marine life, a source of vital resources, and a critical zone for human activities such as fishing, oil exploration, and underwater research. However, we also confront the challenges and vulnerabilities the continental shelf ecosystems face, as human activities and environmental pressures impact their delicate balance.

Exploring the Depths - The Mysterious Oceanic Abyss

Now we discover the depths of the oceanic abyss, the enigmatic realm that stretches beyond the reach of sunlight. We contemplate the mesmerizing mysteries of the mesopelagic and aphotic zones, where darkness and cold prevail and life adapts to extreme conditions. We marvel at the remarkable creatures that thrive in these deep-sea environments, illuminating our understanding of the incredible biodiversity beneath the surface. Exploring the depths of the oceans, we deeply appreciate their vastness, diversity, and the intrinsic connection between their geography and the web of life they sustain.

As we journey across the oceanic landscapes, we're left in awe by these vast aquatic territories' stunning splendor and deep-seated importance. They shape our planet's surface, influence its climate, and provide a home to an astonishing array of life

Overview of the Coverage of the Oceans on Earth

The vast and majestic oceans blanket our planet with their awe-inspiring expanse. In this section, we embark on an enlightening overview of the coverage of the oceans on Earth, delving into their immensity and the significance they hold for our planet and all life it supports.

The Dominance of the Oceans

As we contemplate the Earth's surface, we are captivated by the overwhelming dominance of the oceans. Oceans encompass more than 70% of the planet's surface and shape our world's fabric. Their vastness stretches across continents, from expansive coastlines to remote and unexplored regions, forging an interconnected network of water that unites nations, cultures, and ecosystems.

The Five Oceanic Basins

Our exploration leads us to the five major oceanic basins of the world ocean: the Atlantic, Pacific, Indian, Southern, and Arctic Oceans. Each basin possesses unique characteristics, vastness, and marine life, sculpted by the interplay of currents, tides, and geological forces. From the Atlantic's grandeur to the immensity of the Pacific, from the remote Southern Ocean to the frozen Arctic waters, we uncover each oceanic basin's remarkable diversity and distinctiveness.

The Interconnectedness of the Oceans

Beyond their individual distinctions, the oceans are interconnected, forming a global system that transcends boundaries. Powerful oceanic currents, such as the Gulf Stream and the Antarctic Circumpolar Current, circulate vast volumes of water, redistributing heat, nutrients, and marine life on a global scale. We inspect the intense interconnectedness of the oceans, recognizing that what happens in one oceanic basin can have far-reaching effects on others, influencing climate patterns,

31

ecosystems, and the overall health of our planet.

Remote and Unexplored Realms

Despite remarkable advancements in ocean exploration, vast expanses of the oceans remain remote and unexplored. The depths of the abyssal plains, the underwater mountain ranges, and the mysterious trenches that plunge to the deepest points on Earth continue to captivate our curiosity. We reflect on the unknown domains beneath the surface, recognizing the vast potential for discovery and the importance of continued exploration to unravel the mysteries in these untouched corners of the oceans.

Explanation of Point Nemo: The Furthest Point of Inaccessibility in the Ocean

In our exploration of the geography of the oceans, we encounter a fascinating and remote location that holds a unique distinction within the vast expanse of the sea: Point Nemo. Point Nemo is renowned as the furthest point of inaccessibility in the South Pacific Ocean, a place of remarkable solitude and seclusion from human presence.

Geographic Location

Point Nemo, also known as the Oceanic Pole of Inaccessibility, is located at coordinates 48°52.6'S latitude and 123°23.6'W longitude. Its precise location lies approximately 2,688 kilometers (1,670 miles) equidistant from the nearest lands: Ducie Island (part of the Pitcairn Islands), Motu Nui (part of the

Easter Island group), and Maher Island (part of Antarctica). It is nestled within the depths of the South Pacific Gyre, a region characterized by vast expanses of open ocean and minimal human activity.

The Significance of Isolation

Point Nemo's isolation results from its great distance from any landmass, making it remarkably lonely and secluded. Its unique geographic location starkly contrasts the bustling coastlines and populated islands that dot other regions of the world's oceans. Point Nemo's isolation has earned it the reputation of being the most remote location on Earth, far removed from the reaches of civilization and human presence.

Scientific and Environmental Importance

Point Nemo's remote location and isolation make it an ideal site for various scientific and environmental endeavors. Its distance from land minimizes the influence of human activity, providing an unpolluted environment that can serve as a reference point for studying the impact of human presence on other parts of the ocean. Furthermore, the region's deep waters and unique ecological conditions make it an intriguing area for marine research, allowing scientists to investigate marine biodiversity, oceanic processes, and the impacts of climate change.

The Spacecraft Cemetery

Point Nemo has gained additional recognition as the final resting place for decommissioned spacecraft. Due to its remote location and minimal risk of human encounters, space agencies deliberately target this area for the controlled re-entry and disposal of satellites, space stations, and other space debris. Here, remnants of human exploration and technological advancements find their eternal resting place in the ocean's depths, far from inhabited areas and the risk of collision with active satellites.

Reflections on Point Nemo

Point Nemo serves as a reminder of the vastness and solitude within the world's oceans. It captivates our imagination, evoking a sense of wonder and curiosity about the mysteries beneath the surface. This remote and inaccessible location encourages contemplation of the relationship between humanity and the vastness of the natural world. It reminds us of our responsibility to preserve and protect the fragile ecosystems that thrive in the oceans, even in the most remote corners, such as Point Nemo.

8

The Ocean's Layers

The Division of the Ocean into Vertical and Horizontal Zones

As we journey into the heart of the ocean's enigmatic layers, we uncover an astounding framework that aids our comprehension of its extensive ecosystems and ecological processes: the division of the ocean into vertical and horizontal zones. This intriguing concept illuminates the intricate habitats in the marine world, offering insights into life's distribution, the varying physical conditions, and the dynamic interplay between different oceanic regions.

Oceanographers have distinguished unique zones based on varying physical and biological properties by examining the ocean's vertical dimension. The pelagic zone, a vast, open expanse that extends from the surface to the ocean floor, forms the backbone of the ocean's water column. Within this vast expanse, further sub-divisions emerge, each defined by depth and light penetration, giving birth to realms such as the photic and aphotic zones.

Commencing at the ocean's surface, the photic zone, where light intensity reaches just 1% of surface value, allows for photosynthesis. Plants and microscopic algae convert light, water, carbon dioxide, and nutrients into organic matter. Forming the primary food source for various organisms and playing a vital role in supporting the ocean's rich biodiversity, this region teems with life.

Venturing deeper beyond the photic zone, we encounter the mesopelagic and aphotic zones. The mesopelagic also called the twilight zone, is characterized by a gradual reduction in light levels, yet houses a diverse array of marine life uniquely adapted to low-light conditions. Descending further into the aphotic zone, we find ourselves enveloped in darkness. This mysterious realm is home to extraordinary lifeforms despite its chilling temperatures and stark darkness. These organisms evolved to thrive under extreme pressure and scarcity of resources and embody the resilience of life within the ocean's depth.

Meanwhile, the horizontal dimension offers us a different perspective of the ocean. Here, the ocean is divided into major bodies of water or seas, each enclosed partially or fully by land. The Mediterranean, Caribbean, and Red Seas have unique geographical features, currents, and ecosystems, each painting a distinct picture of marine life. Adding further to this rich tapestry are the marginal and inland seas lying along continental edges and partially enclosed by landmasses.

Exploring these vertical and horizontal zones helps us under-stand the multifaceted yet beautifully interconnected marine environments. They provide a robust framework for conserving the ocean's ecosystems while unraveling the secrets of adaptation and survival in various oceanic regions. Every zone provides a window into the diverse and complex marine life, offering a deeper appreciation of the resilience and marvel of organisms thriving in the ocean's vast aquatic realm. As we peel back the layers of the ocean, we're reminded of the enchanting mysteries that remain hidden within each zone.

9

Oceanic Temperatures and Currents

Factors Affecting Ocean Temperatures

As we delve into the fascinating world of oceanic temperatures, we encounter many factors that influence the heat distribution within the vast ocean. Understanding these factors allows us to comprehend the complex dynamics of temperature variations and their impact on marine life, climate patterns, and global oceanic circulation.

Solar Radiation

Solar radiation plays a fundamental role in determining ocean temperatures. The amount of sunlight absorbed by the ocean's surface directly affects its heating. Near the equator, where sunlight is more direct, the ocean experiences higher temperatures. As we move towards the poles, the sun's angle decreases, resulting in lower temperatures. Variations in solar radiation throughout the year, influenced by the Earth's axial tilt and seasonal changes, contribute to the cyclical nature of oceanic temperature patterns.

Latitude and Geographical Position

Latitude and geographical position have a profound impact on ocean temperatures. Regions closer to the equator, characterized by lower margins, tend to experience warmer temperatures due to their proximity to the sun's direct rays. In contrast, higher latitudes near the poles receive less solar radiation, resulting in cooler temperatures. The oceanic temperature gradient across spaces contributes to the formation of global climate patterns and drives the circulation of ocean currents.

Oceanic Currents

Ocean currents, driven by various forces such as wind, temperature differences, and the Earth's rotation, significantly influence ocean temperatures. Currents act as conveyer belts, transporting warm or cold water from one region to another. Warm ocean currents, such as the Gulf Stream, carry heat from the equatorial regions to higher latitudes, raising the temperatures of coastal areas. Conversely, cold ocean currents, like the California Current, bring cooler waters from the polar regions, leading to lower temperatures along their paths.

Land-Sea Interactions

The proximity of landmasses to the ocean can influence local temperature patterns. Coastal areas are subject to the moderating effect of the ocean, which can regulate temperature extremes. Land-sea breezes, generated by differential heating between land and water, can impact coastal temperatures. During the day, the land heats faster than the ocean, leading to onshore breezes and cooler temperatures. At night, the reverse occurs, resulting in offshore breezes and relatively warmer temperatures.

By comprehending the factors contributing to oceanic temperature variations, we gain insights into the complex interplay between the sun, currents, and geographical features. These temperature dynamics shape climate patterns, influence marine habitats, and drive the mechanisms of the Earth's hydrosphere. Exploring the depths of oceanic temperatures unveils the delicate balance and interconnectedness of the world's oceans, inspiring us to appreciate the large impact these factors have on the fragile equilibrium of our planet.

Explanation of Major Ocean Currents and Their Roles in Global Climate

Ocean currents, powerful and dynamic, play a crucial role in shaping the Earth's climate system. In this section, we dive into the depths of major ocean currents, exploring their pathways and understanding their significant contributions to global climate patterns.

The Gulf Stream

One of the most prominent and well-known ocean currents, the Gulf Stream, flows along the eastern coast of North America before turning northeastward toward Europe. Originating in the Gulf of Mexico, this warm and swift current transports vast amounts of heat from the tropics to higher latitudes, influencing the climate of both regions. The Gulf Stream's warm waters contribute to the temperate climate of Western Europe, making it milder than other areas at similar latitudes.

The Kuroshio Current

The Kuroshio Current, flowing northward along the eastern coast of Asia, is Japan's equivalent of the Gulf Stream. Originating in the Philippine Sea, this warm, fast-moving current carries heat from the tropics to the western North Pacific Ocean. Its influence extends beyond temperature regulation, shaping the region's climate and supporting diverse marine ecosystems.

The Agulhas Current

The Agulhas Current, located along the eastern coast of South Africa, is a warm and powerful western boundary current. Originating from the Indian Ocean, it transports warm water southward, parallel to the coast. The Agulhas Current influences regional climate, providing heat and moisture for nearby land areas. It also plays a role in the global thermohaline circulation, contributing to the movement of warm surface waters toward the poles.

The Antarctic Circumpolar Current

The Antarctic Circumpolar Current, encircling Antarctica, is the world's largest ocean current. This cold and swift eastward-flowing current connects the Atlantic, Indian, and Pacific Oceans, serving as a vital link between the major oceanic basins.

41

The Antarctic Circumpolar Current influences global climate by transferring large amounts of cold water from the Southern Ocean to lower latitudes, affecting temperature distributions and regulating atmospheric carbon dioxide levels.

Oceanic Upwelling and Downwelling

Upwelling and downwelling phenomena impact oceanic temperatures, particularly in coastal areas. Upwelling occurs when cold, nutrient-rich waters rise to the surface, replacing warmer surface waters. This process promotes cooler temperatures and enhances marine productivity by bringing nutrient-laden waters from the depths. Downwelling, on the other hand, involves sinking surface waters, often associated with the convergence of currents or the formation of deep-ocean circulation patterns. Downwelling can lead to the transfer of heat from the surface to deeper layers, affecting temperature distributions.

The interactions of these major ocean currents and upwelling and downwelling processes contribute to the complex and interconnected system known as the global thermohaline circulation. This system is vital in distributing heat around the planet, influencing regional climates, and impacting weather patterns. The ocean's immense heat capacity and the movement of oceanic currents act as a giant heat reservoir, helping to moderate temperature extremes, regulate atmospheric conditions, and shape the Earth's climate locally and globally.

As we demystify the sophisticated web of major ocean currents and their significant impact on global climate, we fully appreciate the complex interplay between the oceans, atmosphere, and land. These currents serve as the essential engines behind climate variability, sculpting weather systems and dictating the transfer of heat and moisture across the globe. Grasping this delicate equilibrium and the interdependencies among these currents prompts us to acknowledge the oceans' influence on our climate. It further underscores the urgent necessity to protect and manage these water bodies sustainably, ensuring the health of our planet and the well-being of generations to come.

10

Gas Exchange in the Ocean

Overview of the Dissolved Gases in the Ocean

As we venture into the ocean's depths, we discover a hidden world where gases dissolve in the watery embrace. The ocean, a vast reservoir of dissolved gases, plays a crucial role in global biogeochemical cycles and the delicate balance of Earth's atmosphere. This chapter explores the fascinating array of gases that find solace within the ocean's depths.

Oxygen

Oxygen is one of the most vital gases present in the ocean. Through photosynthesis, marine plants and algae release oxygen into the water, allowing it to dissolve and support the respiration of marine organisms. Dissolved oxygen is essential for the survival of marine life, providing the energy required for metabolic processes and maintaining the delicate balance of ecosystems.

Carbon Dioxide

Carbon dioxide, a greenhouse gas, is also present in the ocean in dissolved form. Carbon dioxide enters the ocean through various processes, including respiration and the dissolution of atmospheric CO2. The ocean serves as a significant sink for carbon dioxide, helping to regulate its concentration in the atmosphere and mitigate the impacts of climate change. However, increasing carbon dioxide levels due to human activities have led to ocean acidification, altering the delicate pH balance and posing challenges for marine organisms and ecosystems.

Nitrogen

Nitrogen is another crucial gas found in the ocean. It enters the water through various sources, including atmospheric deposition, rivers, and nitrogen-fixing organisms. Dissolved nitrogen is vital in supporting primary productivity and the growth of marine plants and algae. It is an essential nutrient for aquatic organisms, contributing to marine ecosystems' overall health and balance.

Other Gases

The ocean also contains other dissolved gases, albeit in smaller concentrations. These include methane, hydrogen sulfide, and various trace gases. Certain microorganisms in oxygen-depleted environments, such as wetlands and marine sediments, can produce methane, a potent greenhouse gas. Hydrogen sulfide, with its characteristic pungent odor, can be present in oxygen-deficient regions, such as oxygen minimum zones or near hydrothermal vents.

The concentrations of dissolved gases in the ocean vary spatially and temporally, influenced by temperature, salinity, biological activity, and gas exchange with the atmosphere. The solubility of gases in seawater depends on these factors, with colder water generally having a higher capacity for gas dissolution. Understanding the dynamics of gas exchange in the ocean is crucial for studying the impacts of climate change, assessing marine ecosystem health, and predicting the response of marine organisms to environmental changes.

Venturing into the world of dissolved gases in the ocean allows us to discern the complex interconnections between the marine world, the atmosphere, and the myriad organisms that inhabit the ocean's depths. The ocean's dual function as a reservoir and regulator of dissolved gases underscores its pivotal role within the Earth's climate framework. Exploring the mechanisms and patterns of gas exchange in the ocean enriches our understanding of our planet's functionality and the intricate interplay of its multifaceted ecosystems.

Discussion on Ocean Acidification Due to Increased Carbon Dioxide Concentration

Ocean acidification, a consequence of rising carbon dioxide (CO2) atmospheric concentrations, poses significant challenges to the delicate balance of marine ecosystems. In this section, we study the phenomenon of ocean acidification, exploring its causes, impacts, and potential implications for marine life.

When excess CO2 from human activities is absorbed by the ocean, a chemical reaction occurs, decreasing seawater pH. This process alters the ocean's carbonate chemistry and reduces the concentration of carbonate ions. These carbonate ions are crucial for forming calcium carbonate, a building block for marine organisms, including corals, shellfish, and phytoplankton.

The repercussions of ocean acidification are far-reaching. One of the most notable impacts is the degradation of coral reefs, which are highly sensitive to changes in pH levels. As the ocean becomes more acidic, corals struggle to build and maintain their calcium carbonate skeletons, leading to coral bleaching, reduced growth rates, and increased vulnerability to other stressors. The loss of coral reefs has intense implications for the biodiversity and resilience of marine ecosystems, as they provide essential habitats for a vast array of marine species.

Ocean acidification also affects shell-forming organisms, such as oysters, clams, and certain plankton species. These organisms rely on calcium carbonate to form their shells or protective exoskeletons. Decreasing carbonate availability compromises their ability to build and maintain these structures, making them more susceptible to predation, disease, and reduced survival rates. This disruption in the marine food web can have cascading effects on entire ecosystems, impacting fisheries, coastal economies, and the livelihoods of communities dependent on marine resources.

Furthermore, ocean acidification can affect the physiology and behavior of marine organisms. Studies suggest that acidification can impair sensory and metabolic functions, alter growth rates, and reduce reproductive success in various species. These changes in physiological processes can disrupt ecological interactions and compromise the overall health and stability of marine ecosystems.

Addressing the issue of ocean acidification requires concerted efforts to mitigate CO_2 emissions and reduce the amount of carbon dioxide entering the atmosphere. Implementing sustainable practices, transitioning to cleaner energy sources, and protecting marine habitats are crucial steps toward safe-guarding the health of our oceans. Additionally, research and monitoring programs are vital for understanding the impacts of acidification on marine ecosystems and informing conservation strategies.

By recognizing the profound impact of ocean acidification on marine life, we are compelled to take action to preserve the delicate balance of our oceans. Through collective responsibility and sustainable practices, we can mitigate the risks posed by increasing carbon dioxide concentrations and protect the diverse and vibrant ecosystems that rely on the health of our oceans.

11

The Ocean's Rich Biodiversity

Examination of the Diverse Species Living in the Ocean

The ocean, an awe-inspiring realm of wonder, harbors a staggering array of life forms. In this chapter, we embark on a journey to explore the rich biodiversity that thrives beneath the waves, uncovering the extraordinary diversity of species that call the ocean their home.

The oceanic environment supports many organisms, ranging from the tiniest microorganisms to colossal marine mammals. Phytoplankton, microscopic algae that harness the power of sunlight through photosynthesis, form the foundation of the marine food web. These microscopic organisms, along with their counterparts, zooplankton, nourish a vast array of marine life, including fish, invertebrates, and even larger predators.

Countless species have adapted to various habitats and ecosystems within the ocean's depths. Coral reefs, vibrant and teeming with life, house an astonishing diversity of marine species. These delicate ecosystems support many colorful fish, corals, crustaceans, and other invertebrates. Coral reefs are biodiversity hotspots and serve as natural coastal barriers, protecting shorelines from erosion and storm damage.

The open ocean, or pelagic zone, is a vast expanse where migratory species roam and elusive creatures dwell. Majestic marine mammals, such as whales, dolphins, and seals, traverse great distances, undertaking remarkable migrations across ocean basins. These magnificent creatures captivate our imagination and remind us of the interconnectedness of life in the ocean.

The deep sea, a realm shrouded in darkness and extreme conditions, harbors mysterious and often bizarre organisms. Strange-looking fish, bioluminescent creatures, and unique adaptations abound in this extraordinary habitat. Venturing into the depths reveals astonishing discoveries, such as hydrothermal vent communities, where life thrives without sunlight, relying on chemosynthesis to harness energy from chemical reactions.

The ocean is estimated to be home to over 230,000 identified species, with countless more yet to be discovered. From tiny plankton to immense whales, from delicate corals to resilient deep-sea organisms, the ocean's biodiversity is a testament to the resilience and adaptability of life. Each species plays a vital role in maintaining the health and balance of marine ecosystems, contributing to processes such as nutrient cycling, carbon sequestration, and the overall functioning of the planet.

However, the ocean's rich biodiversity faces numerous threats, including habitat degradation, overfishing, pollution, and the impacts of climate change. Human activities have put immense pressure on marine ecosystems, compromising the delicate balance of life beneath the waves. Through scientific exploration, conservation initiatives, and raising awareness, we can appreciate the awe-inspiring diversity of life in the ocean and work towards preserving it for future generations.

Impact of Human Activity on Ocean Ecosystems, Including Pollution and Overfishing

The delicate equilibrium of ocean ecosystems, with their complex life network, is progressively undermined by human endeavors. In this segment, we explore the significant implications of human-induced activities on the vitality and endurance of ocean ecosystems, spotlighting key issues such as pollution and overfishing.

Pollution

Human-generated pollution has become a significant threat to the oceans and the organisms that depend on them. Industrial and agricultural runoff, coastal development, and improper waste disposal have accumulated harmful substances in marine environments. Chemical pollutants, including heavy metals, pesticides, plastics, and oil spills, contaminate the water and pose serious risks to marine life. These pollutants can disrupt reproductive systems, impair growth and development, and even cause mortality in aquatic organisms. Additionally, plastic debris, which takes centuries to degrade, accumulates in marine ecosystems, endangering marine species through entanglement and ingestion.

Overfishing

Overfishing, driven by commercial demand and unsustainable fishing practices, has severely depleted fish populations worldwide. Large-scale fishing operations, including bottom trawling and longlining, indiscriminately capture vast amounts of marine life, often resulting in the depletion of target species and collateral damage to non-target species. Removing key predator species disrupts the balance of marine food webs, leading to cascading effects throughout the ecosystem. Overfishing also impacts the livelihoods of coastal communities that rely on fish stocks for food security and economic stability.

Habitat Destruction

Human activities, such as bottom trawling, coastal development, and destructive fishing practices, destroy critical marine habitats. Physical damage, sedimentation, and pollution threaten coral reefs, seagrass meadows, mangrove forests, and other essential ecosystems. The loss and degradation of these habitats jeopardize the survival of numerous species that depend on them for food, shelter, and reproduction. The destruction of coastal habitats also leaves shorelines vulnerable to erosion and storm damage, putting human communities at risk.

Climate Change

The ocean is intricately linked to Earth's climate system, and human-induced climate change is altering oceanic conditions at an alarming rate. Rising sea temperatures, ocean acidification, and sea-level rise significantly affect marine ecosystems. Warmer waters disrupt marine species' distribution and behavior, causing range shifts and impacting their reproductive cycles. Ocean acidification threatens the growth and survival of organisms that rely on calcium carbonate structures, such as corals and shellfish. Additionally, sea-level rise poses risks to coastal habitats and communities, increasing the vulnerability of coastal ecosystems and exacerbating the impacts of storms and flooding.

Mitigating the Impacts

Addressing these challenges requires concerted efforts to mitigate pollution, promote sustainable fishing practices, protect critical habitats, and reduce greenhouse gas emissions. Implementing stricter regulations and adopting innovative technologies can help reduce pollution inputs into the oceans. Sustainable fisheries management involves establishing marine protected areas and utilizing ecosystem-based approaches to support the recovery of fish stocks and protect marine biodiversity. Conservation initiatives aimed at restoring and preserving critical habitats are essential for maintaining the resilience and functionality of marine ecosystems. Additionally, reducing greenhouse gas emissions and transitioning to cleaner energy sources can help mitigate the impacts of climate change on the oceans.

By recognizing the detrimental effects of human activities on ocean ecosystems, we can take collective action to promote responsible stewardship of these vital environments. Preserving the health and biodiversity of the oceans is crucial for the survival of marine species and the well-being of human communities that depend on the oceans for food, livelihoods and cultural identity. Through sustainable practices, awareness campaigns, and international cooperation, we can work towards a future where the oceans thrive, ensuring the preservation of our planet's most valuable ecosystems.

12

Legends of the Deep

Exploration of Various Oceanic Legends and Myths

Throughout history, the vast and enigmatic oceans have sparked the human imagination, giving rise to many captivating legends and myths. In this chapter, we set sail on a voyage to untangle the tales interwoven into the rich fabric of maritime folklore, enveloping us in the sense of wonder and enigma that pervades the depths.

One of the most enduring legends of the sea is that of the Kraken, a colossal sea creature believed to dwell in the deep ocean. Described as a massive, tentacled beast capable of capsizing ships, the Kraken has captured the imaginations of sailors and storytellers for centuries. Legends of encounters with this mythical creature have been passed down through generations, adding an air of mystique to the vast expanses of the ocean.

The fabled Lost City of Atlantis, often depicted as an advanced and prosperous civilization submerged beneath the sea, has fascinated explorers and scholars for ages. The ancient Greek philosopher Plato described Atlantis as a utopian society that met its tragic fate in a cataclysmic event. The story of Atlantis continues to captivate our imagination, prompting quests for its discovery and inspiring countless literary and artistic works.

Tales of sea monsters have been prevalent in maritime folklore across cultures. From the sea serpents of Norse mythology to the mythical Leviathan and the legendary sea dragons of Asian legend, these captivating creatures embody the unknown and untamed aspects of the ocean. They symbolize the power and untapped mysteries that lie beneath the waves.

The enchanting allure of sirens and mermaids has bewitched seafarers throughout history. These mythical creatures, often depicted as half-human and half-fish, embody both beauty and danger. Legends tell of their mesmerizing songs that lured sailors to their doom or their benevolent presence guiding lost souls to safety. The tales of sirens and mermaids blur the lines between fantasy and reality, stirring our fascination with the ocean's secrets.

The legend of the Flying Dutchman, a ghost ship doomed to sail the seas for eternity, has become an enduring symbol of maritime lore. The ghostly vessel said to be crewed by tormented souls, is believed to be an omen of misfortune and doom to those who encounter it. The tale of the Flying Dutchman speaks to the mysteries of the ocean and the timeless stories of lost souls trapped between the realms of the living and the dead.

56

These oceanic legends and myths reflect our deep-seated fascination with the unknown and our desire to make sense of the sea's vast and often treacherous realm. They serve as a testament to the enduring power of storytelling and the human need to weave narratives that explore the uncharted territories of our imagination. While these legends may originate from fantasy, they evoke a sense of wonder and ignite our curiosity about the wonders beneath the waves.

Immersing ourselves in the enthralling narratives of the deep, we begin to grasp the cultural importance embedded within these legends, transcending boundaries and generations. They serve as poignant reminders of the deep-rooted bond between humanity and the ocean, evoking a range of emotions and instilling an appreciation for the aquatic domain's immeasurable power and enigmatic wonders. These timeless tales of the deep fuel our relentless quest for exploration, igniting our imagination and nurturing an unbreakable connection with the vast and captivating world that is the ocean.

The legends and myths surrounding the ocean have allowed humans to grapple with the mysteries and complexities of this vast and untamed realm. These tales offer a glimpse into the connection between humanity and the enigmatic world beneath the waves. The ocean, with its vastness and hidden depths, has always been a source of wonder and awe. Legends such as the Kraken and sea monsters symbolize the unfathomable creatures that inhabit the depths, which remain largely unexplored and mysterious. These tales reflect our fascination with the unknown and our deep-seated desire to unravel the secrets beneath the surface. They remind us that despite our advancements in science and technology, hidden wonders and creatures still defy our understanding.

The myth of Atlantis, a lost city beneath the sea, speaks to the allure of hidden civilizations and submerged landscapes. It represents the notion that beneath the waves, there may exist ancient ruins and forgotten worlds waiting to be discovered. The legend of Atlantis taps into our collective imagination. It fuels our desire to explore and unravel the mysteries of the ocean's depths.

Sirens and mermaids, with their seductive songs and mythical allure, capture the beauty and danger that coexist in the marine world. These legends highlight the captivating power of the ocean and its ability to mesmerize and enthrall. They evoke a sense of enchantment and mystery, reminding us of the unfathomable wonders that lie beneath the waves.

The tale of the Flying Dutchman and other ghostly apparitions at sea reflects the sense of mystery and the inherent risks associated with maritime exploration. These legends embody the ethereal and often treacherous nature of the ocean, reminding us of the dangers and uncertainties that sailors and explorers have faced throughout history. They serve as a reminder of the vastness and unpredictability of the ocean, leaving room for the unexplained and the supernatural.

As the ocean's mysteries intertwine, the oceanic legends evoke a sense of reverence and respect for the power and complexity of the maritime realms. They inspire exploration and curiosity, urging us to delve deeper into the unknown and uncover the truths beneath the waves. While these tales may be rooted in folklore and mythology, they speak to our deep connection with the ocean and our innate desire to seek answers and make sense of the world.

Conclusion

The Wonder and Responsibility of Oceans

Throughout our exploration of the oceans, we've marveled at their beauty, ecological significance, and significant mysteries. From climate regulation to cultural importance, the oceans are essential to our planet and well-being.

The oceans are our life support system covering over 70% of the Earth's surface. They produce oxygen, regulate temperatures, and absorb carbon dioxide. They provide valuable resources and serve as trade, transportation, and cultural exchange avenues. The oceans are a source of inspiration, recreation, and solace for countless people.

However, our oceans face numerous challenges. Pollution, overfishing, climate change, and habitat destruction threaten their delicate balance. Our responsibility as custodians of the Earth is to protect and preserve these invaluable ecosystems.

To safeguard the oceans, we must adopt sustainable practices. Minimizing pollution, promoting responsible fishing, and reducing our carbon footprint are crucial steps. Conservation and restoration efforts should focus on critical habitats like coral reefs, mangroves, and seagrass meadows. Embracing renewable energy sources and international cooperation in addressing climate change is vital.

Education and awareness are crucial in fostering stewardship and appreciation for the oceans. Understanding our interconnectedness with them inspires action. Citizen science initiatives, marine research support, and community-driven conservation efforts make a difference.

Our responsibility to the oceans extends beyond our lifetime. It's a commitment to future generations and the sustainability of our planet. We can forge a harmonious relationship with the oceans by embracing this responsibility.

Call to Action for Ocean Preservation

The oceans' plight demands immediate action. We call upon individuals, communities, governments, and organizations to safeguard the oceans.

Raise Awareness: Share knowledge, educate, and promote dialogue about the oceans' value and vulnerabilities.

Reduce Pollution: Embrace sustainable practices, recycle, minimize single-use plastics, and support responsible waste management.

Promote Sustainable Fisheries: Choose certified sustainable seafood, advocate for fishing regulations, and support sustainable aquaculture.

Protect Critical Habitats: Recognize the importance of

coastal ecosystems, coral reefs, mangroves, and seagrass meadows. Support initiatives and engage in community-led conservation efforts.

Mitigate Climate Change: Support renewable energy, reduce greenhouse gas emissions, and advocate for climate action.

Foster International Collaboration: Encourage global cooperation in marine research, policy development, and conservation efforts.

Support Ocean Research and Conservation: Back organizations dedicated to marine research, contribute to citizen science initiatives, and volunteer or donate to projects focused on ocean protection.

Together, we can make a difference. Let's ensure the oceans thrive, biodiversity flourishes, and their immeasurable value is respected. The time to act is now. Together, we can be the guardians our oceans need.

Participate in the Discovery: Please Share Your Thoughts

Thank you for diving into the depths with us in "The Abyss Below: Astonishing Ocean Facts & Legends - An In-depth Exploration of Our Planet's Watery Realms." We hope you've enjoyed the deep-sea exploration as much as we enjoyed bringing the mysteries of our oceans to the surface.

Your thoughts and reflections are invaluable to us and future marine explorers. Please take a moment to leave a review on Amazon. Share with us - and potential readers - your experience navigating the book. Which facts left you astonished? Did you come across any intriguing legends you'd like to discuss? Your feedback helps us refine our future works and guides fellow readers as they select their next underwater adventure.

Leaving a review is easy. Just visit the book's page on Amazon, navigate to the 'Customer Reviews' section, and click 'Write a customer review.' Your insight could be the lighthouse guiding others toward the mysteries of our ocean depths.

Resources

Ballard, R.D. (2001). Lost Liners: From the Titanic to the Andrea Doria, the Ocean Floor Reveals Its Greatest Ships. Hyperion.

Clendenning, A. (2021). Twenty fun facts about the ocean. *BYUH Ke Alaka'i*. https://kealakai.byuh.edu/twenty-fun-facts-about-the-ocean

Cousteau, J.Y. (1953). The Silent World: A Story of Undersea Discovery and Adventure. Harper & Brothers.

Earle, S.A. (2010). The World Is Blue: How Our Fate and the Ocean's Are One. National Geographic.

Ellis, R. (1998). The Empty Ocean: Plundering the World's Marine Life. Island Press.

Gessner, D. (2019). The Book of Atlantis Black: The Search for a Sister Gone Missing. Tin House Books.

Hohn, D. (2019). Moby-Duck: The True Story of 28,800 Bath Toys Lost at Sea and of the Beachcombers, Oceanographers, Environmentalists, and Fools, Including the Author, Who Went in Search of Them. Penguin Books.

McPhee, J. (1997). The Founding Fish. Farrar, Straus and Giroux.

Montgomery, S. (2015). The Soul of an Octopus: A Surprising Exploration into the Wonder of Consciousness. Atria Books.

Safina, C. (2016). The View from Lazy Point: A Natural Year in an Unnatural World. Henry Holt and Company.

Team, T. (2023). 10 Unbelievable Facts about the Ocean. *Real Word*. https://www.trafalgar.com/real-word/10-unbelievable-facts-ocean/

Top 10 things you didn't know about the ocean | U.S. Geological Survey. (n.d.). https://www.usgs.gov/programs/cmhrp/news/top-10-things-you-didnt-know-about-ocean

Wikipedia contributors. (2023c). Ocean. *Wikipedia*. https://en.wikipedia.org/wiki/Ocean

Winchester, S. (2010). Atlantic: Great Sea Battles, Heroic Discoveries, Titanic Storms, and a Vast Ocean of a Million Stories. Harper Perennial.

www.ingramcontent.com/pod-product-compliance
Lightning Source LLC
Chambersburg PA
CBHW071037050426
42335CB00051B/2364